Problem Solving & Reasoning Activity Book

for ages 10-11

This CGP book is bursting with fun activities to build up children's skills and confidence.

It's ideal for extra practice to reinforce what they're learning in primary school. Enjoy!

Published by CGP

Editors:
Mary Falkner, Ruth Greenhalgh, Jake McGuffie, Sean McParland and Claire Plowman

With thanks to Alison Griffin and Julie Wakeling for the proofreading.

With thanks to Jade Sim for the copyright research.

ISBN: 978 1 83774 068 0

Printed by Elanders Ltd, Newcastle upon Tyne.
Clipart on the cover and throughout the book from Corel®
Cover design concept by emc design ltd.

Text, design, layout and original illustrations © Coordination Group Publications Ltd. (CGP) 2024
All rights reserved.

Photocopying this book is not permitted, even if you have a CLA licence.
Extra copies are available from CGP with next day delivery • 0800 1712 712 • www.cgpbooks.co.uk

Contents

Adding and Subtracting — 2

Multiplying and Dividing — 4

Calculating with Decimals — 6

Fractions — 8

Fractions, Decimals & Percentages — 10

Relative Sizes and Sharing — 12

Puzzle: Bug Fixin' — 14

Algebra — 16

Measurement — 18

Perimeter, Area & Volume — 20

Shapes and Angles — 22

Data, Charts & Graphs — 24

Mixed Problems — 26

Answers — 28

Adding and Subtracting

How It Works

Sometimes you might need to do some addition and subtraction to solve a problem. You'll need to read the question carefully and break it up into steps. Take a look at this example:

A company made 469 296 pens last year. 192 561 were blue pens and 123 421 were red pens. How many pens were not blue or red?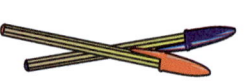

First add together the number of blue and red pens that the factory made... ...then subtract this from the total number of pens that they made.

```
  1 9 2 5 6 1
+ 1 2 3 4 2 1
  ─────────
  3 1 5 9 8 2
          1
```

```
       8 12
  4 6 9̶ 2̶ 9 6
−   3 1 5 9 8 2
  ─────────
    1 5 3 3 1 4
```

Now Try These

1. On one day, the highest temperature in Hamar, Norway, was −12 °C. The highest temperature in Rundu, Namibia, was 31 °C. How much warmer was Rundu than Hamar?

.... °C

2. Super Squirrel collected 236 512 nuts for winter. Nutbad, the squirrel villain, stole 96 447 of them. Then Super Squirrel collected another 113 222 nuts. How many nuts does Super Squirrel have now?

I have .... nuts!

3. Lovisa bought a sandwich for £6.25 and a lemonade for £1.89.
   She also bought a slice of cake, which was £3.15 cheaper than the sandwich.

   a) Estimate how much Lovisa spent.

   £ ....

   b) Lovisa paid with a £20 note.
      How much change did she get?

   £ ....

4. Mr Dobbs has three sausage dogs, Haggis, Salami and Banger.
   Haggis is 63.7 mm shorter than Salami. Banger is 31.3 mm longer than Haggis.
   If Salami is 612.5 mm long, how long is Banger?

   .... mm

An Extra Challenge

Emma the decorator makes her own paint colours by mixing yellow, red, blue and white paint. Here are her instructions for making four of her colours:

Mango Mist	Sea Green	Cherry Blossom	Lime Dream
To make 1 tin, mix:	To make 1 tin, mix:	To make 1 tin, mix:	To make 1 tin, mix:
1552 ml yellow	1269 ml blue	1527 ml white	1317 ml yellow
405 ml red	456 ml yellow	690 ml red	710 ml blue
543 ml white	775 ml white	283 ml yellow	473 ml white

Emma had 3000 ml of yellow paint. She made one tin each of two of the paint colours above.
If she has 1227 ml of yellow paint left now, which two colours did she make?
How much white paint did she use?

Have you got addition and subtraction all worked out?

Multiplying and Dividing

How It Works

You can multiply and divide numbers using mental maths if you can see how the numbers link to times tables facts. For example, 70 × 3000 = (7 × 3) × 10 × 1000 = 210 000.

But if the numbers are more tricky, you'll have to use a written method such as long multiplication, short division or long division. Here are a couple of examples:

Long multiplication

```
              5 7 9 2
         ×       3 5
5792 × 5 →   2 8 9 6 0
               3 4 1
5792 × 30 → 1 7 3 7 6 0
               2 2
Add to get → 2 0 2 7 2 0
the answer.  1 1 1 1
```

Long division

```
              3 4 8 r 2
          24 | 8 3 5 4
24 × 3 = 72 → − 7 2 ↓
                1 1 5
24 × 4 = 96 → − 9 6 ↓
                  1 9 4
24 × 8 = 192 → − 1 9 2
                      2
```

The remainder is 2.

Now Try These

1. A shop sells 8000 boxes of paperclips every year.
   Use mental maths to work out how many paperclips they sell if each box contains:

   a) 50 paperclips

   .... paperclips

   b) 400 paperclips

   .... paperclips

2. Fill in the missing digits in these calculations.

```
       ☐ 9 3 4
   ×        8 3
     5 ☐ 0 2
       2 1 1
   1 5 4 7 ☐ 0
       7 2 3
   1 6 ☐ 5 2 2
       1 1
```

```
              8 ☐ 4 r ☐
         12 | 9 ☐ 9 1
             − 9 6 ↓
                 2 9
               − 2 ☐
                   5 1
                 − 4 8
                      ☐
```

3. Miss Mack the maths teacher lives on a street with houses numbered from 1 to 80. Her house number is a common multiple of 3 and 8. It is also one less than a prime number. What house number does Miss Mack live at?

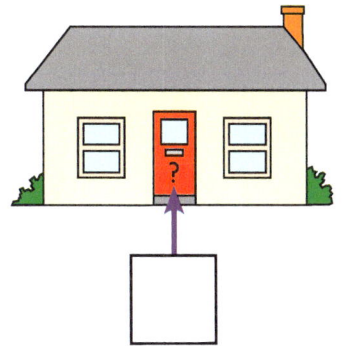

4. Kenny is making giant garden gnomes. He needs 27 kg of clay to make each one. If he has 6546 kg of clay, how many giant gnomes can he make?

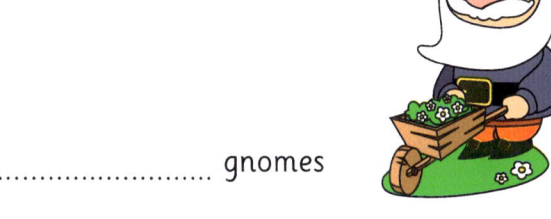

.... gnomes

5. A library has 14 rooms of books. Each room has 112 shelves. Each shelf can hold 36 books. If all the shelves are full, how many books does the library have?

.... books

An Extra Challenge

Monsterville town council is holding a big barbecue for all the monsters who live there.

Their plan is shown on the right.

How many packs of bread rolls do they need to buy?

Big Barbecue Plan

- There are 28 327 monsters living in Monsterville. We want everyone to come!
- We want to allow 14 sausages for each monster. Each sausage will be served in a bread roll.
- Bread rolls come in packs of 24.

Are you a multiplication master? And a dab hand at division?

Calculating with Decimals

How It Works

If you're multiplying or dividing a decimal by 10, 100 or 1000, you can just carefully move the digits. For example:

O t
3.5 × 100 =
H T O
350

To multiply by 100, move all the digits two places to the left.

If it's a more complicated calculation, use written multiplication or division. Do a whole-number calculation and then work out where the decimal point needs to go. Here are some examples:

39.1 ÷ 17

First do 391 ÷ 17. You could use short or long division.

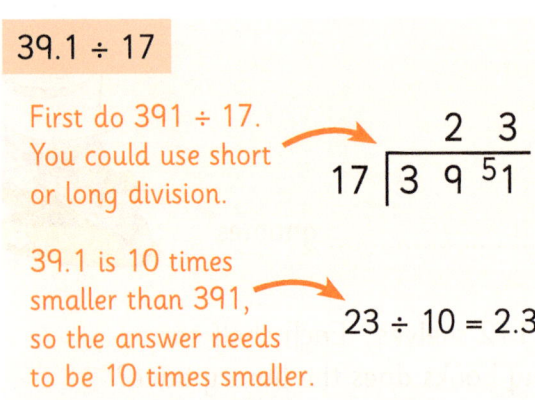

39.1 is 10 times smaller than 391, so the answer needs to be 10 times smaller.

23 ÷ 10 = 2.3

3.12 × 14

First do 312 × 14.

3.12 is 100 times smaller than 312, so the answer needs to be 100 times smaller.

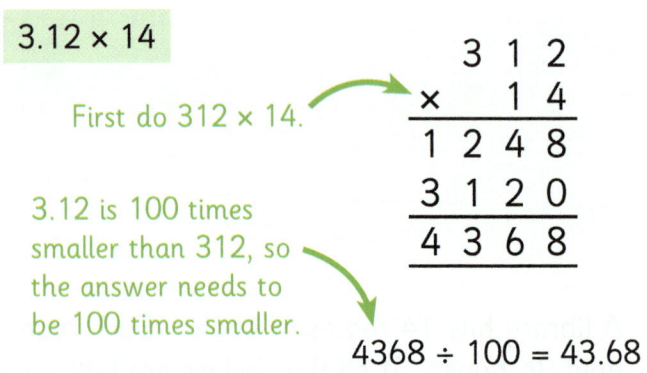

4368 ÷ 100 = 43.68

Now Try These

1. A part of each of these calculations has been covered up.

   Draw lines to match each calculation to its missing part on the right.

 21.5 = 215

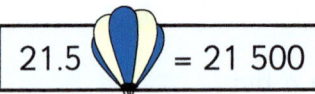 21.5 = 0.215

 21.5 = 21 500

 21.5 = 2.15

21.5 = 2150

× 1000

÷ 100

× 100

÷ 10

× 10

2. Dom the dragon has 211.5 litres of fireberry squash. If he shares it out equally between 15 dragons, how many litres of squash will everyone get?

.... litres

3. Sarah makes cushions. To make each one, she needs 0.72 m of red fabric and the same amount of purple fabric. How much fabric will she need in total to make 27 cushions?

.... m

4. Look at the vases on the right.
   What is the total cost, rounded to the nearest 10p, of:

   a) 3 small vases?   b) 12 large vases?

£5.62

£8.21

£ ....   £ ....

5. Amit has a roll of ribbon that is 12.75 m long. First he uses 2.55 m of it to tie up a parcel. Then he cuts the remaining ribbon into 12 pieces that are all the same length. How long will each piece be, in metres?

.... m

An Extra Challenge

Kacey put a decimal number into the function machine shown below.

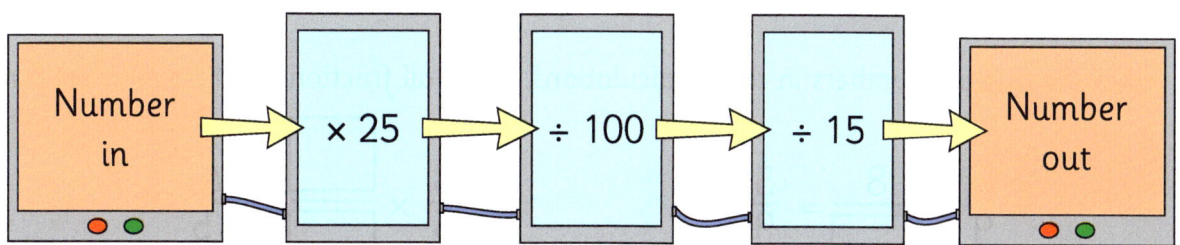

The number that Kacey got out of the machine was 0.56. What number did Kacey put into the function machine? What number would she get out if she put in 6.6?

Have you got the point of working with decimals?

7

Fractions

How It Works

To compare fractions, first use equivalent fractions to get them over the same denominator — then compare the numerators. Have a look at this example:

Which is bigger, $\frac{3}{4}$ or $\frac{2}{3}$? $\frac{3}{4} = \frac{9}{12}$ (×3) and $\frac{2}{3} = \frac{8}{12}$ (×4) so $\frac{3}{4}$ is bigger.

You also need fractions to have the same denominator when you add or subtract them.

$\frac{1}{4} + \frac{3}{8} = \frac{2}{8} + \frac{3}{8} = \frac{5}{8}$ (×2)

To multiply fractions, multiply the numerators, then multiply the denominators.

$\frac{2}{5} \times \frac{4}{7} = \frac{8}{35}$

To divide a fraction by a whole number, multiply the denominator by the whole number.

The numerator stays the same.

$\frac{5}{9} \div 3 = \frac{5}{27}$ ← 9 × 3 = 27

Now Try These

1. Mr Skoolseasy's class are doing their maths work when the bell rings for break. "Anyone who has completed $\frac{2}{3}$ or more of their questions can pack up and go out", he says. Circle the notepads of the pupils who can go.

   $\frac{7}{10}$ $\frac{5}{7}$ $\frac{13}{20}$ $\frac{5}{8}$ $\frac{8}{11}$

2. Fill in the missing numbers in these calculations. Give all fractions in their simplest form.

   $\frac{7}{9} \times \frac{8}{\Box} = \frac{56}{99}$ $\frac{3}{5} \times \frac{\Box}{\Box} = \frac{6}{15}$

   $\frac{5}{\Box} \div 4 = \frac{5}{24}$ $\frac{2}{7} \div \Box = \frac{2}{35}$

3. Three teams are doing a treasure hunt. Each team member says what fraction of the clues they were the first on their team to solve.

a) Which team has the most clues still to solve? ....

b) What fraction of the clues does that team have left to solve? ....

4. Some animals are lining up to cross the log bridge over the raging rapids. They must cross one by one, in order from lightest to heaviest.

   a) Number the animals 1 to 6 to show the order in which they should cross.
      Hint: the units are all the same, so don't worry about them.

   Zebra ☐ $\frac{2}{5}$ tonne
   Giraffe ☐ $\frac{9}{10}$ tonne
   Hippo ☐ $2\frac{3}{5}$ tonnes
   Elephant ☐ $6\frac{1}{4}$ tonnes
   Lion ☐ $\frac{7}{40}$ tonne
   Hyena ☐ $\frac{1}{20}$ tonne

   b) The log breaks once it's had 2 tonnes on it. Which animal will fall into the rapids?

   ....

An Extra Challenge

Matty's maths has got all mixed up.
Write the numbers from the cards in the right places to make the calculation correct, using each card once. (None of the fractions are improper.)

Cards: 1 2 2 3 4 7 8

$$\frac{\Box}{\Box} \times \frac{\Box}{\Box} = \frac{\Box}{\Box\Box}$$

Are you feeling a fraction more confident now?

Fractions, Decimals & Percentages

How It Works

Converting a fraction to a decimal is easy if the fraction can be written with a denominator of 10 or 100.

$\frac{35}{100}$ = 35 hundredths = 0.35

$\frac{3}{10}$ = 3 tenths = 0.3

You might be able to use equivalent fractions to get a denominator of 10 or 100.

$\frac{9}{20} = \frac{45}{100} = 0.45$ (× 5)

Or you can convert any fraction to a decimal by dividing the numerator by the denominator:

$\frac{5}{8} = 5 \div 8$ → $8 \overline{)5.^{5}0^{2}0^{4}0}$ = 0.625, So $\frac{5}{8} = 0.625$

A percentage is just a fraction of 100. For example: 35% = 35 out of 100 = $\frac{35}{100}$

To find percentages of amounts, it's often best to start by finding 10% — just divide by 10. Then use that to find the percentage you need. E.g. to find 15% of 40:

10% of 40 = 40 ÷ 10 = 4. 5% is half of 10%, so 5% = 4 ÷ 2 = 2, and 15% = 4 + 2 = 6.

Now Try These

1. The game Unicorns and Dragons is about a herd of 60 unicorns and a clan of 80 dragons. Each round, a unicorn card and a dragon card are drawn — the card that describes the largest number of creatures wins. Circle the winner of each round below.

   30% of the unicorn herd have golden glitter.   25% of the dragon clan breathe blue fire.   **1**

   unicorns / dragons

   55% of the unicorn herd have rainbow manes.   40% of the dragon clan have emerald scales.   **2**

   unicorns / dragons

2. Eoin has $\frac{7}{8}$ kg of brown rice and 0.53 kg of white rice. He puts all of his rice into a bowl, then weighs the full bowl on some scales. The scales read 1.787 kg. How much would the bowl weigh if it were empty? Give your answer as a decimal.

   .... kg

3. Geraint is having a sale. He'd like all the bags in his shop to cost less than £10 but more than £6. Which of these offers would work for all the bags? Tick the correct box(es).

30% off   25% off

20% off

4. Parvati is training for the 100 m sprint. Her coach records her best time at the end of each month. "You have improved by $\frac{2}{10}$ of a second every month," he tells her.

   a) Her best time in January was 14.8 seconds.
      What were her best times for the next three months?

      Feb: .... seconds   Mar: .... seconds   Apr: .... seconds

   b) When she competes in a race she is beaten by $\frac{15}{100}$ of a second.
      The winning runner records a time of 14.3 seconds.
      What was Parvati's time in the race?

      .... seconds

An Extra Challenge

Malia is crossing the squelchy swamp. She can only step on tree stumps that are equivalent to each other. Can you find the three possible routes she can take through the swamp?

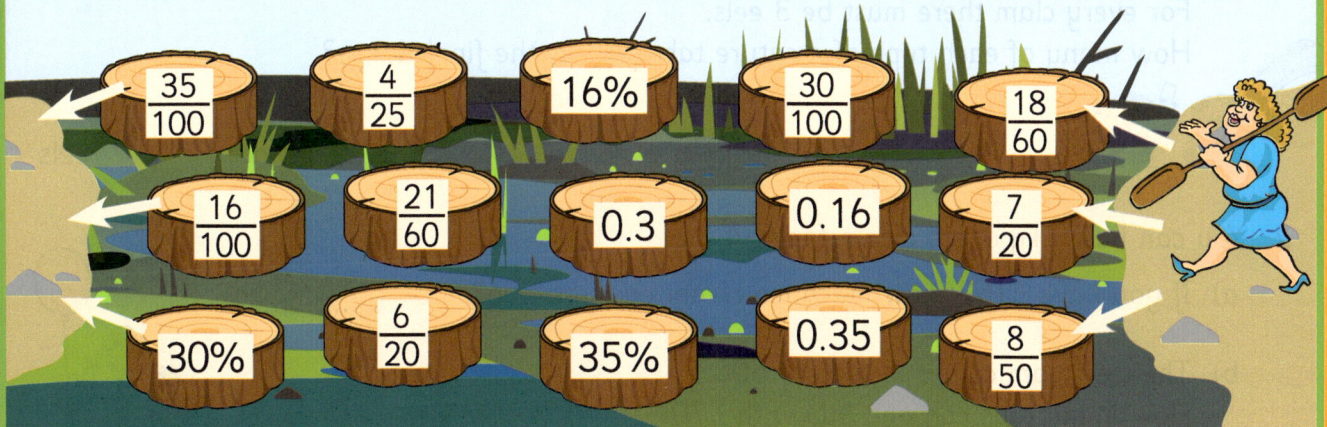

Tick the face that is equivalent to your feelings on this topic...

Relative Sizes and Sharing

How It Works

When two quantities are always in the **same ratio**, multiply or divide to scale them up or down. For example:

To make Perfect Purple paint, you need 2 litres of red paint for every 3 litres of blue paint.

a) Tammy uses 8 litres of red paint. How much blue paint should she use?

8 litres is 8 ÷ 2 = 4 lots of 2 litres, so she should use 3 × 4 = 12 litres of blue paint.

If you know the total quantity and want to divide it into **unequal parts**, first find the total number of parts.

b) Kian makes 60 litres of purple paint. How much red paint does he use?

There are 2 + 3 = 5 parts in total. So there are 60 ÷ 5 = 12 litres in one part. Multiply to find the amount of red paint: 12 × 2 = 24 litres of red paint. (And 12 × 3 = 36 litres of blue paint).

When a shape is **enlarged**, all the lengths are multiplied by the same number, called the **scale factor**. For example:

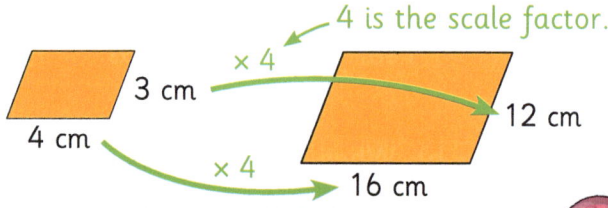

4 is the scale factor.

Now Try These

1. At the annual under-the-sea ball, the sea creatures group up for each dance.

   a) The samba requires 3 jellyfish for every 2 octopuses.
   If there are 18 octopuses dancing, how many jellyfish are there?

   ....

   b) The final dance involves a total of 80 sea creatures — clams and eels.
   For every clam there must be 3 eels.
   How many of each type of creature take part in the final dance?

   .... clams   .... eels

2. You can buy 9 kg of ice cream for £54.

   a) If you have £162, how much ice cream can you buy?   .... kg

   b) The ice cream comes in tubs of 500 g.
   How many tubs can you buy with £70?

   .... tubs

3. The pirates on the Happy Dodger have some rules about any treasure they find.

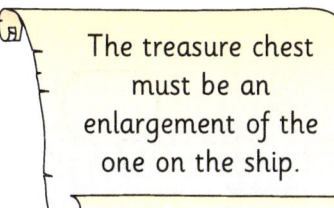
The treasure chest must be an enlargement of the one on the ship.

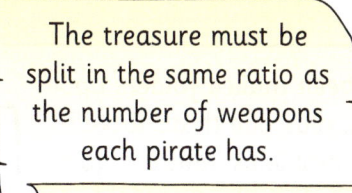
The treasure must be split in the same ratio as the number of weapons each pirate has.

a) Circle the treasure chest below that they take.

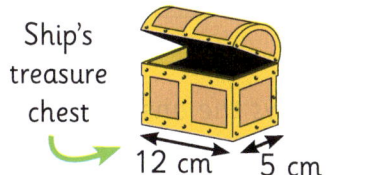
Ship's treasure chest
12 cm   5 cm

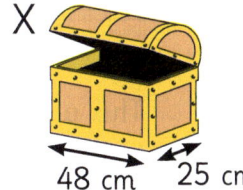
X
48 cm   25 cm

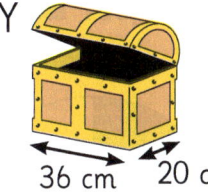
Y
36 cm   20 cm

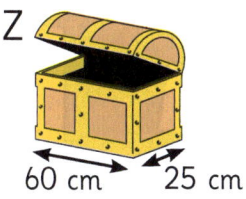
Z
60 cm   25 cm

b) Jimbob gets 24 jewels. How many jewels does Captain Thursty get?

Jimbob

Captain Thursty gets .... jewels.

4. The same scale factor has been used to make a series of enlargements on the fish below. What was it? ....

5 cm   ×?   ×?   ×?   135 cm

An Extra Challenge

Layla has three pet sharks. She catches 120 fish for their dinner.
She needs to divide the fish between them, but they're quite fussy — these are their rules:

- They only like to eat whole fish.
- The smallest shark must get 4 times fewer fish than the middle shark.
- The biggest shark must get twice as many fish as the other two sharks put together.

How many fish does each shark get?

Are you relatively happy with scaling and sharing?

Bug Fixin'

The Bug Fixers have been mailed folders upon folders of broken files, plus one that's locked itself up... Fix all the problems, and use your answers to help them unlock the final folder.

problem_001

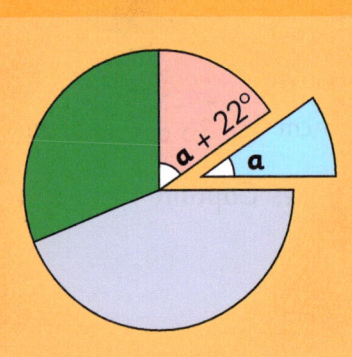

This pie chart shows the answers to an online survey.

The sectors without labels represent $\frac{3}{4}$ of the survey answers.

What is the value of **a**? ....°

problem_002

The following sequence has been corrupted, so all the terms are cycling between fractions, percentages and decimals.

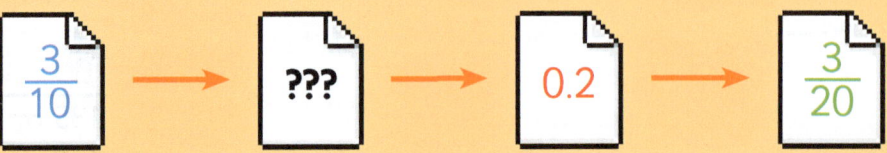

What is the missing number in the sequence? .... %

problem_003

The calendar app icon seems unusually big... it must have been enlarged.

Before the app icon was enlarged, it had an overall height of 3 cm.

What was the height of the '2' **before** the app icon was enlarged? .... cm

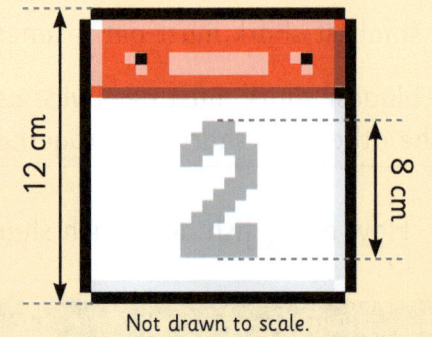

Not drawn to scale.

problem_004

The device code has been encrypted, and the Bug Fixers need to find the original code.

DEVICE CODE: 94861-**XXXXX**

ENCRYPTED CODE: 38150-24967

The code is split into two 5-digit numbers. It was encrypted by subtracting the same amount from both 5-digit numbers.

What number is **XXXXX**? ....

problem_005

The printer app is getting the dimensions of the paper it uses wrong.

The long edge of a piece of A4 paper is 297 mm long, but the printer app thinks it is 11 times **smaller**.

The short edge of a piece of A4 paper is 210 mm, but the printer app thinks it is a **third** of that.

What does the printer app think the **area** of a sheet of A4 paper is? .... mm²

cat_photos

The locked folder of cute cat photos is password protected. Use the numbers you wrote down earlier to generate a password and unlock the folder.

004 − (001 + 002 + 003 + 005)

cats

The password to the folder is: ☐ ☐ ☐ ☐ ☐

Algebra

How It Works

You can use symbols or letters to solve problems involving **missing numbers**, for example:

I'm thinking of a number. I multiply it by 2 and then add 3. The answer is 13.

Start by calling the missing number 'm'... → m × 2 + 3 = 13 (or 2m + 3 = 13)
... then subtract 3 from both sides... → m × 2 = 10
... and divide both sides by 2 to find m. → m = 5

You can also find **pairs of values** that work in problems, for example:

2y − z = 10, where y and z are positive whole numbers. Find a pair of possible values for y and z.

If y = 8... 2y − z = 10
2 × 8 − z = 10
16 − z = 10 ... so z = 6.

You can write **formulas** to find one quantity if you know another, for example:

When Hassan makes paper flowers, he makes 6 petals for every flower, plus 3 spare petals. Write a formula for the total number of petals he makes for any number of flowers.

number of petals = 6 × number of flowers + 3

If he is making 8 flowers, how many petals will he make in total? 6 × 8 + 3 = **51 petals**

Now Try These

1. Jordan has a ribbon that is r cm long. He cuts 2 cm off each end, so that the piece of ribbon he has left is 15 cm long.

   a) Use this information to write an equation involving r.

   Equation: ....

   b) Use your equation to work out the value of r.

   .... cm

2. Maddy works in a chocolate factory. She makes three batches of chocolate bars, with ⬤ bars in each batch. After she has taken 6 bars away for testing, she is left with 54 chocolate bars in total.

   Write an equation involving ⬤, then find the number of bars in each batch.

   Equation: ....

   ⬤ = ...

3. Asher invites some friends to his birthday party.

   a) When he buys balloons, he gets 3 balloons for each guest, plus 10 spare. Write a formula for the number of balloons he needs to buy for any number of guests.

   ....

   b) There are 25 guests coming to his party. How many balloons does he need?

   .... balloons

   c) Asher wants to give everyone either a bouncy ball or a key ring in their party bag. So he can decide how many of each to buy, he writes the rule r + b = 25, where 'r' is the number of key rings and 'b' is the number of bouncy balls.

   Fill in the missing numbers in the table.

Key rings	Bouncy balls
10	
	9
18	

   d) At the party, the number of songs sung as karaoke (k) multiplied by the number of songs played by the DJ (d) equals 100, so that k × d = 100.

   If there are more than 3 and fewer than 20 karaoke songs, write down all the possible pairs of numbers of songs there could have been.

   .... karaoke songs and .... DJ songs

   .... karaoke songs and .... DJ songs

   .... karaoke songs and .... DJ songs

An Extra Challenge

Aalia is making patterns out of shapes. Here are the first three she makes.

She compares the number of purple rectangles with the number of the pattern and starts writing a formula:

number of purple rectangles = number of pattern...

- What should Aalia write to finish the formula?
- Which pattern will have 30 purple rectangles?

How it works + solving problems + checking answers =

Measurement

How It Works

You can convert metric units:

For mass:
1 kg = 1000 g

For length:
1 cm = 10 mm
1 m = 100 cm
1 km = 1000 m

For volume:
1 litre = 1000 ml

For time:
1 minute = 60 seconds
1 hour = 60 minutes
1 day = 24 hours
1 week = 7 days
1 year = 365 days

Leap years have 366 days.

To convert from a bigger unit to a smaller unit, multiply by the conversion factor. E.g. 2.5 kg = 2.5 × 1000 = 2500 g.

To go from a smaller unit to a bigger unit you need to divide by the conversion factor. E.g. 357 cm = 357 ÷ 100 = 3.57 m.

You can also change between metric and imperial units.

For length:
1 inch ≈ 2.5 cm

For distance:
5 miles ≈ 8 km

'≈' means 'approximately equal to'

Now Try These

1. Sofia is a scientist working in a desert. She measures four different cactuses. Here are her results:

   Cactus 1: 2982 mm
   Cactus 2: 122 inches
   Cactus 3: 295 cm
   Cactus 4: 2.87 m

   Which cactus is the tallest?

   Cactus ....

2. A group of people and their camels are trekking across the desert from Tala to Jeb. The route is shown here.

   Tala — 23 km — 15 miles — 91 500 m — Jeb

   a) Approximately how many kilometres will they travel in total?

   .... km

   b) At one point their route is blocked by an extra-large sand dune. They have to go round it, which adds an extra 3.2 km to their journey. Approximately how many miles does it add to their journey?

   .... miles

3. Talia is filling buckets of water. The volume of water in each bucket is shown below.

1.98 litres   1989 ml   2.02 litres   1.95 litres   2030 ml

   a) Circle the bucket that contains the closest to 2 litres.

   b) From the last bucket of water (2030 ml), she pours out 0.032 litres.
      How much is left in the bucket?

   .... ml

4. Ahmed is flying from the Sahara desert to the Kalahari desert and back.
   His flight there lasts for 325 minutes. The journey back includes a
   45 minute stopover in Kampala and lasts 8 hours in total.
   a) How long does Ahmed spend flying on his trip?

   .... hours .... minutes

   b) Alysha takes the same trip, but her flight there is 2400 seconds longer and her flight
      back is 6000 seconds shorter than Ahmed's. How long does she spend flying in total?

   .... hours .... minutes

   c) Adam has been in the Kalahari for 725 days. He is going to stay for 2 years
      and 5 weeks (neither are leap years). How many days has he got left in the Kalahari?

   .... days

An Extra Challenge

Chantelle converted each measurement in the orange boxes to a different unit,
but she spilt ink on her answers and they got all mixed up.
Work out the correct units for the green boxes and match the pairs of equal measurements.

4865 ml   4685 mm   4865 m   4586 l   4568 g   4856 mm

4.865   4 586 000   4.856   4.568   486 500   468.5

How would you measure your
success in this topic?

19

Perimeter, Area & Volume

How It Works

Perimeter is the distance round the edge of a shape.   **Area** is the space inside a shape.

Shapes with the **same areas** can have **different perimeters**, and shapes with the **same perimeters** can have **different areas**.

Each grid square represents 1 cm by 1 cm.

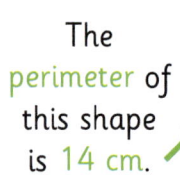
The perimeter of this shape is 14 cm.

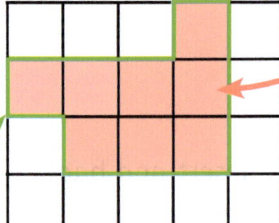
The area of both of these shapes is 8 cm².

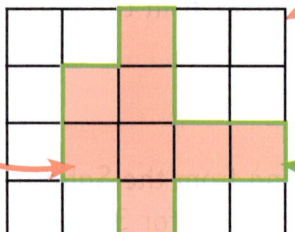
The perimeter of this shape is 16 cm.

You can find the **area** of parallelograms and triangles by using formulas.

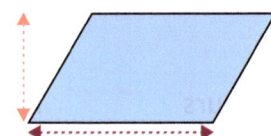
Area = base × height

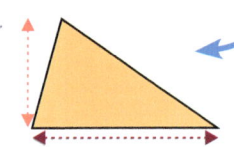
Area = ½ × base × height

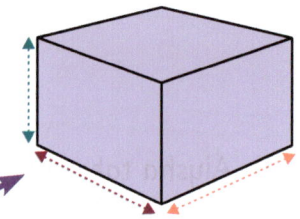

Find the **volume** of cubes and cuboids by using this formula: volume = length × width × height

Now Try These

1. Mia has drawn a shape made from squares on the grid below. Each grid square represents 1 cm by 1 cm.

a) Draw a shape with the same perimeter as Mia's shape but a different area.

b) Draw a shape with the same area as Mia's that has the largest possible perimeter.

c) Draw a shape with the same area as Mia's that has the smallest possible perimeter.

2. TJ has made a large model robot.
   He hasn't painted the back of the robot.
   The diagram on the right shows his design.

   a) The robot's body and legs are cuboids.
      What is their total volume?

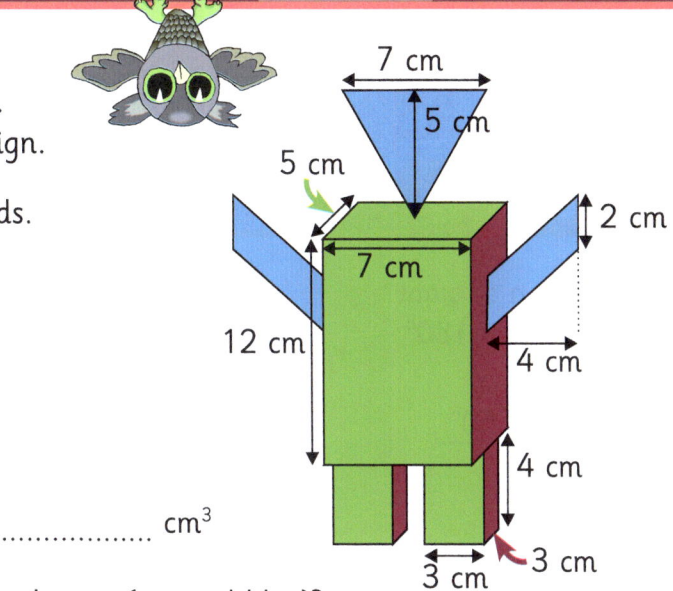

   .... cm³

   b) What is the total area of the head and arms (painted blue)?

   .... cm²

3. Deepa splits a parallelogram into three triangles like this.
   The base of the parallelogram is 10 cm and the height is 4.5 cm. The area of triangle Z is 6.75 cm².

   What are the areas of triangles X and Y?

   X = ... cm²   Y = ... cm²

An Extra Challenge

Look at the three objects below. Some of their dimensions have floated away.
Use the given volumes to match the dimension labels to the correct arrows.
Add an appropriate unit to each dimension and volume.

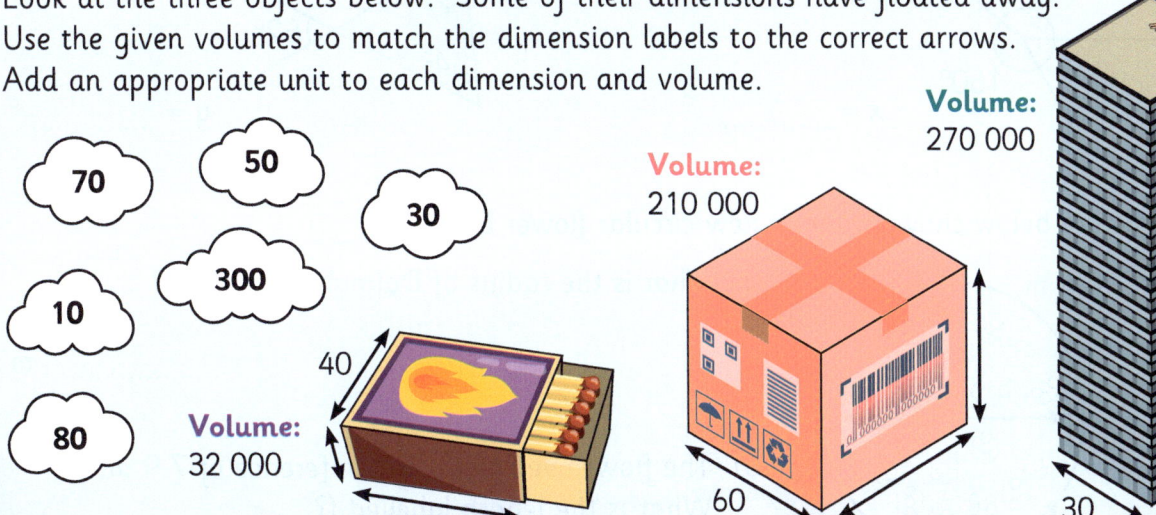

What volume of this topic have you mastered?

Shapes and Angles

How It Works

Angles on a straight line add up to **180°**.

a = 180° − 50° = 30°

Angles around a point add up to **360°**.

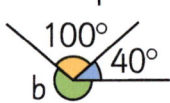

b = 360° − 100° − 40° = 220°

Vertically opposite angles are **equal**.

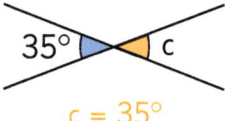

c = 35°

Angles in a triangle add up to **180°**.

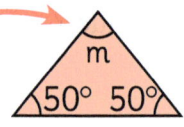

m = 180° − 50° − 50° = 80°

Angles in a quadrilateral add up to **360°**.

n = 360° − 115° − 115° − 65° = 65°

These are the parts of a **circle**:

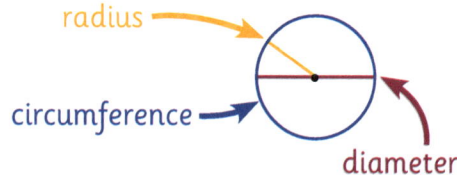

Nets fold up to make 3D shapes. For example:

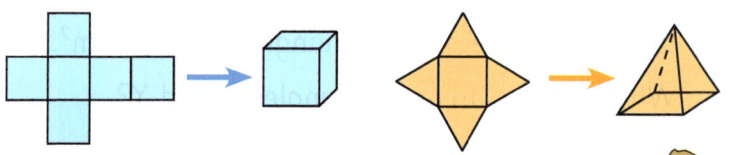

Now Try These

1. Find the missing angles in the diagrams below.

   a)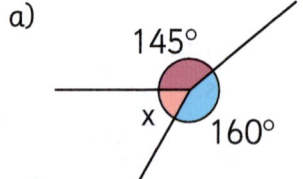

   x = ... °

   b)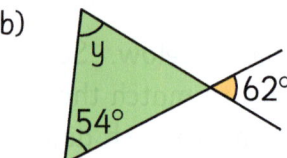

   y = ... °

2. The picture below shows Danny's new circular flower bed.

   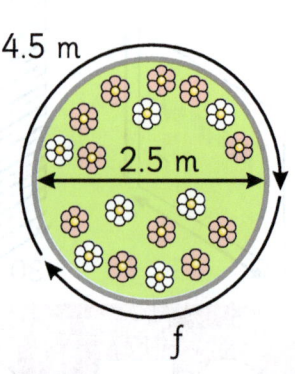

   a) What is the radius of Danny's flower bed?

   .... m

   b) The flower bed has a circumference of 7.9 m. What is the length labelled f?

   .... m

3. The diagram on the right shows the net of an unusual dice. The numbers on opposite faces of the dice should add up to 10.

   Write a number in each empty square to complete the net.

4. Two sides of a rhombus have been drawn on the left. Use a ruler and protractor to accurately complete the rhombus.

5. Deji draws two triangles on a grid, Triangle A and Triangle B.

   Triangle A has vertices (−5, −2), (−7, −5) and (−2, −3).

   When Triangle B is reflected in the y-axis it creates the same image as when Triangle A is reflected in the x-axis.

   Draw and label Triangles A and B on this grid.

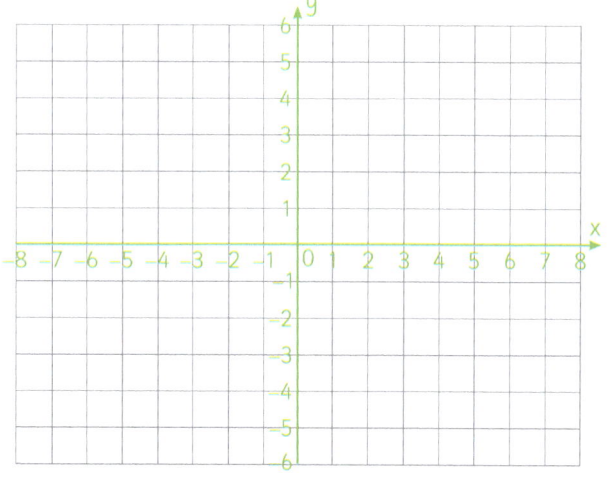

An Extra Challenge

Molly is making a mosaic to decorate her front doorstep. She drew a design for the mosaic, but hasn't worked out all of the angles yet. Find the angles labelled **A-H** for Molly.

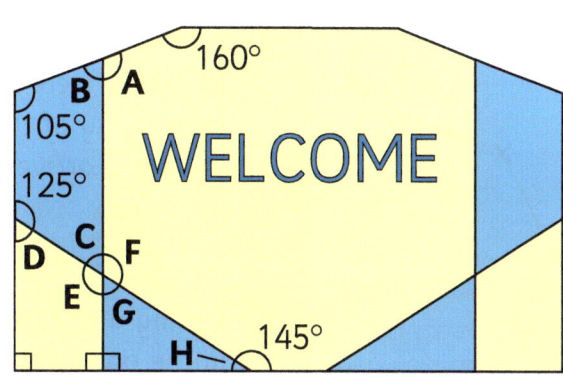

(Not drawn to scale.)

Have you turned a corner with shapes and angles?

23

Data, Charts & Graphs

How It Works

Pie charts and line graphs are both ways of displaying data.

For example, this pie chart shows the favourite colours of the children in Year 6. There are 60 pupils in the class, and 18 pupils said blue.

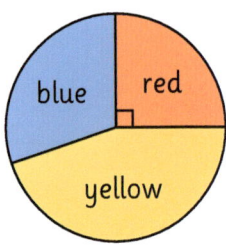

The angles in a pie chart add up to 360°.
So one pupil is worth 360° ÷ 60 = 6°.
So the angle for the 'blue' sector is 18 × 6° = 108°.

The angle for the 'red' sector is 90°.

So $\frac{90}{360} = \frac{1}{4}$ of the pupils said red.

This is 60 ÷ 4 = 15 pupils.

This line graph shows how the depth of water in a river changed over half a day.

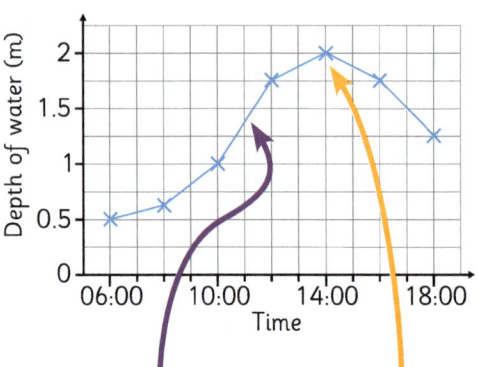

The line is steepest between 10:00 and 12:00, so this is when the depth was changing the fastest.

The deepest the river got was 2 m (at 14:00).

You also need to know about the mean, which is a type of average. To find it, add up all the numbers and then divide that total by how many numbers there are. Here's an example:

Owen's three hamsters weigh 167 g, 160 g and 183 g. What is their mean weight?

167 g + 160 g + 183 g = 510 g   Mean = 510 g ÷ 3 = 170 g

Now Try These

1. A scientist recorded the number of frogs living in a pond over the course of eight years. A line graph of their data is shown below.

a) All the frogs that were living in the pond in Year 1 were still there in Year 3. How many of the frogs recorded in Year 3 arrived after Year 1?

....

b) During a one-year period, 10 frogs arrived in the pond and 4 frogs left it. Between which two years did this change occur?

Year .... and Year ....

24

2. A shop sells three flavours of ice cream. One week it sold 30 chocolate ice creams. It sold 20 more vanilla ice creams than chocolate, and 40 fewer strawberry ice creams than vanilla. Draw a pie chart to show this information.

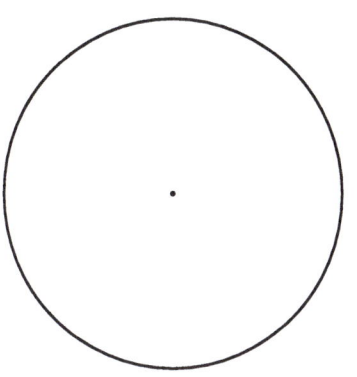

3. The mean time taken for five runners to finish a race is 160 seconds. The times taken by four of the runners are shown below. What is the missing time?

.... s

4. In a survey, 45 people were asked what their favourite vegetable was. This pie chart shows the results. How many people said carrots were their favourite vegetable?

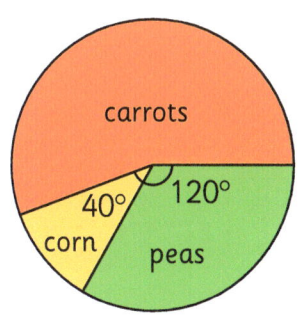

.... people

An Extra Challenge

A group of four friends grew one sunflower each. After they had measured the heights of the flowers, Sean wrote down these notes:

The total height of all four sunflowers is 260 cm.

I forgot to include Maya's sunflower when I worked out the mean. The mean height of the three sunflowers I included was 10 cm less than the mean height of all four sunflowers.

Can you work out the height of Maya's sunflower?

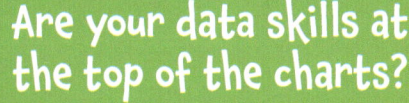

Mixed Problems

How It Works

To solve some problems, you might need to use a mix of different maths skills. For example:

The bases of a regular hexagon and a triangle form a straight line together.
Angle b is 70% of the size of angle a. What are the sizes of angles a and b?

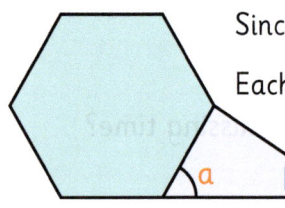

Since the bases form a straight line, angle a is an **exterior angle** of the hexagon.

Each exterior angle of a regular polygon with n sides is $\frac{360°}{n}$.

Each exterior angle of a regular hexagon is 360° ÷ 6 = 60°. So a = 60°.
10% of 60° = 60° ÷ 10 = 6°, so b = 70% of 60° = 6° × 7 = 42°.

If you're doing calculations that involve a mix of operations, remember to use BODMAS — it will make sure that you do everything in the right order.

BODMAS — Brackets, Division, Multiplication, Addition and Subtraction

Here's an example: 5 × (3 + 9) − 10 = 5 × 12 − 10   Then the multiplication.
                                                                5 × 12 = 60
Do the bit in brackets first.   = 60 − 10
3 + 9 = 12   = 50   Do the subtraction last.

Now Try These

1. Work out the answers to these calculations.

   5 × (5 + 7) = ☐   70 + 70 × 30 = ☐

   66 ÷ (6 + 5) − 4 = ☐   23 + (21 + 11) ÷ 8 = ☐

2. The diagram below shows how much pocket money four friends get.

   Mei: £6.50   Paul: £4.25   Anna: £5.30   Kyle: £4.75

   Mei rounds each amount to the nearest pound,
   then calculates the mean of the rounded amounts.

   How much bigger will Mei's answer be than the
   actual mean amount of pocket money?

   £ ....

3. Look at the jars of sweets below. Mrs Jenkins divides up the sweets equally between the 78 pupils in Year 6. How many sweets will each pupil get?

Mega sweet jar
1594 sweets

Big sweet jar
1058 sweets

.... sweets

4. Nora wants to cover a triangular part of her garden with pebbles. She needs 70 kg of pebbles for every 1 m². How many kilograms of pebbles will she need to cover the area shown in the diagram?

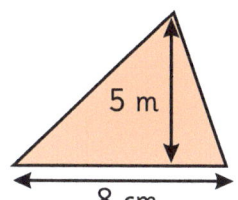
5 m
8 cm

.... kg

5. The pie chart on the right shows the results of a survey about what flavour of pie customers at a cafe liked best. What percentage of the customers liked cherry pie best?

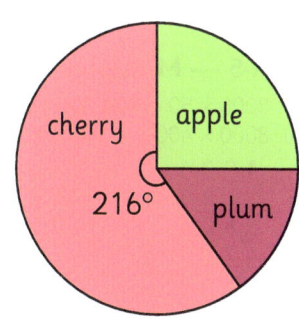
cherry 216° apple plum

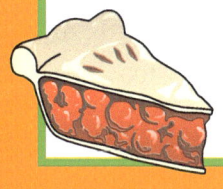

.... %

An Extra Challenge

Hamish, Sandy and Nitesh have all been buying rabbit food for their pets. The packets they bought are shown below — there were special offers on all of them. They bought 4.6 kg altogether. What number should replace the x on Sandy's packet?

Hamish

Usually 1.5 kg, but has 10% extra for free.

Sandy

Usually 1.05 kg, but has x kg extra for free.

Nitesh

Usually 1450 g, but has 100 g extra for free.

Do you have your mixed maths skills in order?

Answers

Pages 2-3 — Adding and Subtracting

1. −12 °C to 0 °C is a jump of 12 °C. 0 °C to 31 °C is a jump of 31 °C. So Rundu was 12 + 31 = **43 °C** warmer.

2.
   ```
     2 3 6 5 7 2        1 4 0 0 6 5
   −   9 6 4 4 7      + 1 1 3 2 2 2
     1 4 0 0 6 5        2 5 3 2 8 7
   ```
   Super Squirrel has **253 287 nuts**.

3. a) E.g. £6 + £2 + (£6 − £3) = £6 + £2 + £3 = **£11**

   b) Cake: Change:
   ```
     6.2 5          2 0.0 0
   − 3.1 5        − 1 1.2 4
     3.1 0            8.7 6
   + 1.8 9
     1 1.2 4
   ```
   So Lovisa got **£8.76** in change.

4. Haggis: Banger:
   ```
     6 1 2.5        5 4 8.8
   −   6 3.7      +   3 1.3
     5 4 8.8        5 8 0.1
   ```
   Banger is **580.1 mm** long.

An Extra Challenge

```
  3 0 0 0         1 3 1 7
− 1 2 2 7       +   4 5 6
  1 7 7 3         1 7 7 3
```
So she used 1773 ml of yellow paint. The yellow paint in **Sea Green** and **Lime Dream** adds up to 1773 ml:

Add up the amount of white paint in **Sea Green** and **Lime Dream**:
```
    7 7 5
  + 4 7 3
  1 2 4 8
```
So she used **1248 ml** of white paint.

Pages 4-5 — Multiplying and Dividing

1. a) 8000 × 50 = **400 000 paperclips**
   b) 8000 × 400 = **3 200 000 paperclips**

2.
   ```
        1 9 3 4           8 2 4 r 3
   ×         8 3     12 ⟌ 9 8 9 1
        5 8 0 2           − 9 6
   1 5 4 7 2 0               2 9
   1 6 0 5 2 2             − 2 4
                                5 1
                             − 4 8
                                 3
   ```

3. The common multiples of 3 and 8 below 80 are 24, 48 and 72. Only 72 is one less than a prime, so Miss Mack lives at **72**.

4.
   ```
        2 4 2 r 12
   27 ⟌ 6 5 4 6
      − 5 4
        1 1 4
      − 1 0 8
            6 6
          − 5 4
            1 2
   ```
   Kenny can make **242 gnomes** (with 12 kg left over).

5. Shelves: Books:
   ```
     1 1 2           1 5 6 8
   ×   1 4         ×    3 6
     4 4 8           9 4 0 8
   1 1 2 0         4 7 0 4 0
   1 5 6 8         5 6 4 4 8
   ```
   There are **56 448 books** in the library.

An Extra Challenge

```
    2 8 3 2 7              1 6 5 2 4 r 2
×         1 4         24 ⟌ 3 9 6 5 7 8
  1 1 3 3 0 8              − 2 4
  2 8 3 2 7 0                 1 5 6
  3 9 6 5 7 8               − 1 4 4
                                1 2 5
                              − 1 2 0
                                    5 7
                                  − 4 8
                                       9 8
                                     − 9 6
                                          2
```
So they need 396 578 bread rolls. 16 524 packs wouldn't be enough, so they need **16 525 packs**.

Pages 6-7 — Calculating with Decimals

1. 21.5 × **10** = 215   21.5 ÷ **10** = 2.15
   21.5 ÷ **100** = 0.215   21.5 × **100** = 2150
   21.5 × **1000** = 21 500

2.
   ```
           1 4 1
   15 ⟌ 2 1 6 1 5
   ```
   141 ÷ 10 = **14.1 litres**

3.
   ```
     0.7 2           1 4 4
   + 0.7 2         ×   2 7
     1.4 4         1 0 0 8
                   2 8 8 0
                   3 8 8 8
   ```
   She needs 1.44 m for each cushion. 3888 ÷ 100 = **38.88 m**

4. a)
   ```
       5 6 2
   ×       3
     1 6 8 6
   ```
   1686 ÷ 100 = £16.86. To the nearest 10p, this is **£16.90**.

   b)
   ```
       8 2 1
   ×     1 2
     1 6 4 2
     8 2 1 0
     9 8 5 2
   ```
   9852 ÷ 100 = £98.52. To the nearest 10p, this is **£98.50**.

5.
   ```
     1 2.7 5              8 5
   −   2.5 5      12 ⟌ 1 0 2 0
     1 0.2 0
   ```
   85 ÷ 100 = **0.85 m**

An Extra Challenge

To find what number Kacey put in, reverse the operations:
56 × 15 = 840, 840 ÷ 100 = 8.4

8.4 × 100 = 840 ⟶
```
       3 3.6
  25 ⟌ 8 4 0.5 0
```
So she put in **33.6**.

66 × 25 = 1650, 1650 ÷ 10 = 165

165 ÷ 100 = 1.65 ⟶
```
          1 1
   15 ⟌ 1 6 5
```
11 ÷ 100 = 0.11 So she would get out **0.11**.

Pages 8-9 — Fractions

1. $\frac{7}{10} = \frac{21}{30} > \frac{20}{30} = \frac{2}{3}$, $\frac{5}{7} = \frac{15}{21} > \frac{14}{21} = \frac{2}{3}$,
   $\frac{13}{20} = \frac{39}{60} < \frac{40}{60} = \frac{2}{3}$, $\frac{5}{8} = \frac{15}{24} < \frac{16}{24} = \frac{2}{3}$,
   $\frac{8}{11} = \frac{24}{33} > \frac{22}{33} = \frac{2}{3}$. So $\frac{7}{10}$, $\frac{5}{7}$ and $\frac{8}{11}$ should be circled.

2. $\frac{7}{9} \times \frac{8}{11} = \frac{56}{99}$, $\frac{3}{5} \times \frac{2}{3} = \frac{6}{15}$, $\frac{5}{6} \div 4 = \frac{5}{24}$, $\frac{2}{7} \div 5 = \frac{2}{35}$

3. a) A: $\frac{4}{16} + \frac{6}{16} + \frac{5}{16} = \frac{15}{16} = \frac{90}{96}$

   B: $\frac{12}{96} + \frac{40}{96} + \frac{33}{96} = \frac{85}{96}$

   C: $\frac{9}{48} + \frac{14}{48} + \frac{16}{48} = \frac{39}{48} = \frac{78}{96}$

   $\frac{78}{96}$ is the smallest fraction, so team **C** has the most to solve.

   b) Total = $\frac{96}{96}$, so they have $\frac{96}{96} - \frac{78}{96} = \frac{18}{96} = \frac{3}{16}$ left.

4. a) In order: $\frac{2}{40}$ (Hyena – **1**), $\frac{7}{40}$ (Lion – **2**), $\frac{16}{40}$ (Zebra – **3**), $\frac{36}{40}$ (Giraffe – **4**), $2\frac{3}{5}$ (Hippo – **5**), $6\frac{1}{4}$ (Elephant – **6**).

   b) Add up the weights of the animals as they cross and look for a total larger than 2 tonnes = $\frac{80}{40}$:

   $\frac{2}{40} + \frac{7}{40} = \frac{9}{40}$, $\frac{9}{40} + \frac{16}{40} = \frac{25}{40}$, $\frac{25}{40} + \frac{36}{40} = \frac{61}{40}$,

   $\frac{61}{40} + 2\frac{3}{5} = \frac{61}{40} + \frac{104}{40} = \frac{165}{40}$. So the total reaches 2 tonnes (and the log breaks) when the **hippo** is crossing.

28

Answers

An Extra Challenge
$\frac{2}{3} \times \frac{4}{7} = \frac{8}{21}$

Pages 10-11 — Fractions, Decimals & Percentages

1. 1: 10% of 60 = 60 ÷ 10 = 6, so 30% = 6 × 3 = 18
   10% of 80 = 80 ÷ 10 = 8, so 5% = 8 ÷ 2 = 4 and
   20% = 8 × 2 = 16. So 25% = 4 + 16 = 20.
   18 < 20, so the **dragons** win.
   2: 10% of 60 = 6, so 5% = 6 ÷ 2 = 3 and
   50% = 6 × 5 = 30. So 55% = 3 + 30 = 33.
   10% of 80 = 8, so 40% = 8 × 4 = 32.
   33 > 32, so the **unicorns** win.

2. $\frac{7}{8}$ = 7 ÷ 8: 8)7.000 = 0.875. So he has 0.875 kg of brown rice.
   He has 0.875 + 0.53 = 1.405 kg of rice, so the empty bowl would weigh 1.787 − 1.405 = **0.382 kg**.

3. 10% of £12 = £12 ÷ 10 = £1.20, so 20% of £12 = £1.20 × 2 = £2.40. So a 20% discount brings the £12 bag to £12 − £2.40 = £9.60.
   The working is similar for the other bags: a 20% discount brings the £9.20 bag to £7.36, and the £8 bag to £6.40. So **20% off** is the correct offer. (Both the other offers bring the £8 bag to less than or equal to £6, so aren't suitable.)

4. a) $\frac{2}{10}$ = 0.2, so her best times were 14.8 − 0.2 = **14.6 seconds** in February, 14.6 − 0.2 = **14.4 seconds** in March and 14.4 − 0.2 = **14.2 seconds** in April.
   b) $\frac{15}{100}$ = 0.15, so her time was 14.3 + 0.15 = **14.45 seconds**.

An Extra Challenge

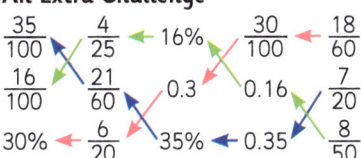

Pages 12-13 — Relative Sizes and Sharing

1. a) 18 ÷ 2 = 9 lots, so there are 9 × 3 = **27 jellyfish**.
   b) 1 + 3 = 4 lots, so 1 lot = 80 ÷ 4 = 20 creatures.
   So 20 × 1 = **20 clams** and 20 × 3 = **60 eels** take part.

2. a) £54 × 3 = £162, so you can buy 9 × 3 = **27 kg**.
   b) 500 g = 500 ÷ 1000 = 0.5 kg. So 1 kg = 2 tubs and 9 kg = 18 tubs. One tub costs £54 ÷ 18 = £3. £70 ÷ £3 = 23 r 1, so you can buy **23 tubs** (with £1 left over).

3. a) 12 × 5 = 60 cm and 5 × 5 = 25 cm, so **Z** is an enlargement with scale factor 5 and should be circled.
   b) Jimbob has 2 weapons and Captain Thursty has 5, so for every 2 jewels Jimbob gets, Captain Thursty gets 5.
   24 ÷ 2 = 12 lots, so Thursty gets 12 × 5 = **60 jewels**.

4. There are 3 enlargements in total, and 135 ÷ 5 = 27, so multiplying by the scale factor 3 times is the same as multiplying by 27. 3 × 3 × 3 = 27, so the scale factor was **3**.

An Extra Challenge
For every fish the smallest shark gets, the middle shark gets 4. So for every 1 + 4 = 5 fish those two sharks get, the biggest shark gets 5 × 2 = 10 fish. (You could write this as 1 : 4 : 10.) There are 1 + 4 + 10 = 15 parts in the ratio, so one part is 120 ÷ 15 = 8 fish. The smallest shark gets **8 fish**, the middle shark gets 8 × 4 = **32 fish** and the biggest shark gets (8 + 32) × 2 = **80 fish**.

Pages 14-15 — Bug Fixin'

problem_001: The labelled sectors represent $1 - \frac{3}{4} = \frac{1}{4}$ of the answers, so the sum of their angles is $360° \times \frac{1}{4}$ = 360° ÷ 4 = 90°.
So a + 22° + a = 2a + 22° = 90°. So 2a = 90° − 22° = 68°.
So a = 68° ÷ 2 = **34°**.

problem_002: 0.2 = $\frac{20}{100}$ and $\frac{3}{20} = \frac{15}{100}$, so the sequence is decreasing by $\frac{20}{100} - \frac{15}{100} = \frac{5}{100}$ each time. $\frac{3}{10} = \frac{30}{100}$, so the missing term is $\frac{30}{100} - \frac{5}{100} = \frac{25}{100}$ as a percentage: **25%**.

problem_003: The scale factor of the enlargement is 12 ÷ 3 = 4. So the height of the '2' was 8 ÷ 4 = **2 cm** before.

problem_004:
```
  8 1
  9 4 8 6 1        So XXXXX − 56 711 = 24 967,     2 4 9 6 7
− 3 8 1 5 0        and XXXXX = 24 967 + 56 711:  + 5 6 7 1 1
  5 6 7 1 1                                        8 1 6 7 8
                                                       1 1
```

problem_005: 297 ÷ 11 = 27 mm, and 210 × $\frac{1}{3}$ = 210 ÷ 3 = 70 mm. So the app thinks the area is 27 × 70 = **1890 mm²**.

cat_photos: 81 678 − (34 + 25 + 2 + 1890)
= 81 678 − 1951 = **79 727**

Pages 16-17 — Algebra

1. a) r − 2 − 2 = 15, so **r − 4 = 15**
   b) Add 4 to both sides: r = **19**

2. Equation: 3◯ − 6 = 54
   3◯ = 54 + 6 = 60, so ◯ = 60 ÷ 3 = **20**

3. a) number of balloons = number of guests × 3 + 10
   b) Substitute 25 for number of guests: 25 × 3 + 10 = **85**
   c) When r = 10: 10 + b = 25, so b = **15**
      When b = 9: r + 9 = 25, so r = **16**
      When r = 18: 18 + b = 25, so b = **7**
   d) 4 × 25 = 100, so **4** karaoke songs and **25** DJ songs
      5 × 20 = 100, so **5** karaoke songs and **20** DJ songs
      10 × 10 = 100, so **10** karaoke songs and **10** DJ songs

An Extra Challenge
number of purple rectangles = number of pattern − **1**
When there are 30 purple rectangles:
30 = number of pattern − 1, so number of pattern = **31**

Pages 18-19 — Measurement

1. Cactus 1: 2982 mm = 2982 ÷ 10 = 298.2 cm
   Cactus 2: 122 inches ≈ 122 × 2.5 = 305 cm
   Cactus 3: 295 cm, Cactus 4: 2.87 m = 2.87 × 100 = 287 cm
   So Cactus **2** is the tallest.

2. a) 15 miles ≈ 15 ÷ 5 × 8 = 3 × 8 = 24 km
      91 500 m = 91 500 ÷ 1000 = 91.5 km
      So total journey ≈ 23 + 24 + 91.5 = **138.5 km**
   b) 3.2 km ≈ 3.2 ÷ 8 × 5 = 0.4 × 5 = **2 miles**

3. a) 1989 ml = 1.989 litres, and 2030 ml = 2.03 litres.
      1.989 litres = **1989 ml** is the closest to 2 litres.
   b) 0.032 litres = 0.032 × 1000 = 32 ml
      2030 ml − 32 ml = **1998 ml**

4. a) Flying time there = 325 minutes = 5 hours 25 minutes
      Flying time back = 45 minutes less than 8 hours
      = 7 hours 15 minutes
      5 hours 25 minutes + 7 hours 15 minutes
      = **12 hours 40 minutes**

Answers

b) 2400 seconds = 2400 ÷ 60 = 40 minutes
6000 seconds = 6000 ÷ 60 = 100 minutes
So overall Alysha's flight is 100 − 40 = 60 minutes
= 1 hour shorter than Ahmed's.
So total flight time = 12 hours 40 minutes − 1 hour
= **11 hours 40 minutes**

c) 2 years 5 weeks = (2 × 365) + (5 × 7) = 730 + 35
= 765 days, so Adam has 765 − 725 = **40 days** left

An Extra Challenge
4856 mm = 4.856 m, 4865 m = 486 500 cm,
4865 ml = 4.865 l, 4685 mm = 468.5 cm,
4586 l = 4 586 000 ml, 4568 g = 4.568 kg

Pages 20-21 — Perimeter, Area & Volume

1. a) Any shape with perimeter = 12 and area not equal to 6, e.g.: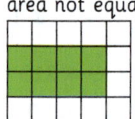
   b) Any shape with perimeter = 14 and area = 6, e.g.: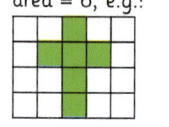
   c) Any shape with perimeter = 10 and area = 6, e.g.: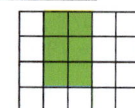

2. a) Body volume = 12 × 7 × 5 = 420 cm³
   Leg volume = 3 × 3 × 4 = 36 cm³
   Total volume of body & legs = 420 + 36 + 36 = **492 cm³**
   b) Area of head = $\frac{1}{2}$ × 7 × 5 = 17.5 cm²
   Area of arm = 2 × 4 = 8 cm²
   Total area of head & arms = 17.5 + 8 + 8 = **33.5 cm²**

3. Area of triangle X: $\frac{1}{2}$ × 10 × 4.5 = **22.5 cm²**
   Area of parallelogram = 10 × 4.5 = 45 cm²
   Area of triangle Y = Area of parallelogram
   − Area of triangle X − Area of triangle Z
   = 45 cm² − 22.5 cm² − 6.75 cm² = **15.75 cm²**

An Extra Challenge
32 000 mm³   210 000 cm³   270 000 m³

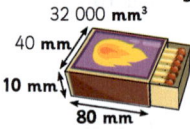  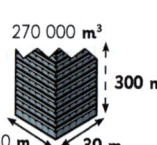

Pages 22-23 — Shapes and Angles

1. a) x = 360° − 145° − 160° = **55°**
   b) Unlabelled angle in triangle = 62°.
   So b = 180° − 54° − 62° = **64°**.

2. a) The diameter = 2.5 m, so the radius = 2.5 ÷ 2 = **1.25 m**.
   b) The circumference = 7.9 m = 4.5 m + f,
   so f = 7.9 − 4.5 = **3.4 m**.

3.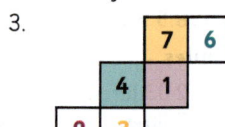

4. (not full size)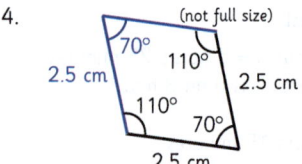
   All sides are of equal length (2.5 cm).
   Opposite angles are equal, and interior angles add to 360°.
   So there are two opposite 70° angles.
   70° × 2 = 140°, so the other two angles add to 360° − 140° = 220°.
   So each is 220° ÷ 2 = 110°.

5. The reflections both make this image.

An Extra Challenge
A = 105°, B = 75°, C = 55°, D = 55°,
E = 125°, F = 125°, G = 55°, H = 35°.

Pages 24-25 — Data, Charts & Graphs

1. a) There were 5 frogs in Year 1, and 13 in Year 3.
   So 13 − 5 = **8 frogs** arrived after Year 1.
   b) 10 − 4 = 6 frogs arrived in total between the two years.
   There were 8 frogs in Year 4 and 14 in Year 5.
   14 − 8 = 6, so the two years are **Year 4 and Year 5**.

2. Chocolate: 30 sold.
   Vanilla: 30 + 20 = 50 sold.
   Strawberry: 50 − 40 = 10 sold.
   30 + 50 + 10 = 90 ice creams sold in total, so each ice cream is worth 360° ÷ 90 = 4°. E.g.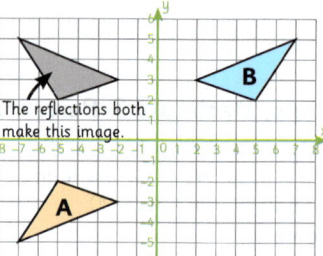

3. Mean time = total time ÷ number of runners
   So total time = mean time × number of runners
   = 160 × 5 = 800 s. 185 + 155 + 150 + 148 = 638 s,
   so the missing time is 800 − 638 = **162 s**.

4. The carrot sector angle is 360° − 40° − 120° = 200°.
   $\frac{200}{360} = \frac{5}{9}$. $\frac{5}{9}$ of 45 = 45 ÷ 9 × 5 = 5 × 5 = **25 people**.

An Extra Challenge
Mean height (of all four) = 260 ÷ 4 = 65 cm.
So the mean height of the three is 65 − 10 = 55 cm.
So the total height of the three is 55 × 3 = 165 cm.
So Maya's sunflower is 260 − 165 = **95 cm**.

Pages 26-27 — Mixed Problems

1. 5 × (5 + 7) = 5 × 12 = **60**
   70 + 70 × 30 = 70 + 2100 = **2170**
   66 ÷ (6 + 5) − 4 = 66 ÷ 11 − 4 = 6 − 4 = **2**
   23 + (21 + 11) ÷ 8 = 23 + 32 ÷ 8 = 23 + 4 = **27**

2. Actual mean amount = total amount ÷ 4
   = (£6.50 + £4.25 + £5.30 + £4.75) ÷ 4 = £20.80 ÷ 4 = £5.20
   Mei's mean = (£7 + £4 + £5 + £5) ÷ 4 = £21 ÷ 4 = £5.25
   So Mei's answer is £5.25 − £5.20 = **£0.05** bigger.

3. ```
     1 5 9 4              3 4
   + 1 0 5 8         78 ) 2 6 5 2
     2 6 5 2            − 2 3 4
         1 1                3 1 2
                          − 3 1 2
                                0
   ```
   So there are 2652 sweets in total. So each pupil gets **34 sweets**.

4. Area = $\frac{1}{2}$ × 8 × 5 = 4 × 5 = 20 m².
   So Nora needs 70 × 20 = **1400 kg** of pebbles.

5. $\frac{216}{360} = \frac{108}{180} = \frac{12}{20} = \frac{60}{100}$ = **60%**

An Extra Challenge
10% of 1.5 kg = 1.5 ÷ 10 = 0.15 kg. So Hamish bought
1.5 + 0.15 = 1.65 kg. Nitesh bought 1450 + 100 = 1550 g
= 1.55 kg. Sandy bought 4.6 − (1.65 + 1.55) = 4.6 − 3.2
= 1.4 kg. So she got 1.4 − 1.05 = **0.35 kg** extra.
   ```